This purchase
was made
possible
with the
Peyton Funds.

SNAKES SET II

YELLOW-BELLIED SEA SNAKES

Adam G. Klein
ABDO Publishing Company

visit us at
www.abdopub.com

Published by ABDO Publishing Company, 4940 Viking Drive, Edina, Minnesota 55435. Copyright © 2006 by Abdo Consulting Group, Inc. International copyrights reserved in all countries. No part of this book may be reproduced in any form without written permission from the publisher. The Checkerboard Library™ is a trademark and logo of ABDO Publishing Company.

Printed in the United States.

Cover Photo: Animals Animals
Interior Photos: Animals Animals pp. 9, 17, 21; Corbis pp. 5, 7, 8, 11, 12, 18; Smithsonian Institution p. 15; Visuals Unlimited p. 19

Series Coordinator: Megan Murphy
Editors: Heidi M. Dahmes, Megan Murphy
Art Direction & Maps: Neil Klinepier

Library of Congress Cataloging-in-Publication Data

Klein, Adam G., 1976-
  Yellow-bellied sea snakes / Adam G. Klein.
     p. cm. -- (Snakes. Set II)
  ISBN 1-59679-281-7
  1. Yellow-bellied sea snake--Juvenile literature. I. Title.

QL666.O64K592 2005
597.96'5--dc22
                                                              2005043333

CONTENTS

YELLOW-BELLIED SEA SNAKES

There are 11 snake **families** in the animal kingdom. The yellow-bellied sea snake, or *Pelamis platurus*, is a member of the Hydrophiidae family. This family is made up of two subfamilies of sea snakes. All sea snakes are **venomous**.

The yellow-bellied sea snake is the most widely traveled snake in the world. It is found in every ocean except the Atlantic. This snake was named because of its bright yellow belly. It is also called the **pelagic** sea snake because it only lives in the ocean.

Whether they live on land or in water, all snakes are vertebrates. They have backbones just like humans. However, snakes are cold-blooded. They must get warmth from outside heat sources. So, the yellow-bellied sea snake only lives in warm ocean waters.

There are two subfamilies of sea snakes, the Hydrophiinae and the Laticaudinae. These subfamilies are further divided into about 50 species of sea snakes.

SIZES

Yellow-bellied sea snakes are medium-sized snakes. Their average length is 25 to 30 inches (65 to 75 cm). The largest yellow-bellied sea snakes can be 44 inches (112 cm) long.

The yellow-bellied sea snake has smooth scales and a thin, sleek body. Its head is long and narrow with large, bulgy eyes. This snake has a long, flat tail that it uses for swimming. Its tail acts as a paddle. When a yellow-bellied sea snake swims, its body moves back and forth.

All snakes shed their skin. Land snakes rub against trees or rocks to help with the shedding process. But, sea snakes don't have much to rub against. So, the yellow-bellied sea snake ties and unties itself into knots. This action helps break off the old skin.

Snakes shed when they outgrow their old skin. Yellow-bellied sea snakes have another reason to shed, too. **Barnacles** and **algae** often attach to their bodies. These creatures slow the snake down a lot. Shedding helps the yellow-bellied sea snake get rid of these pests.

The scales on the yellow-bellied sea snake's belly are smaller than those on a land snake. So, it is almost impossible for a yellow-bellied sea snake to move around on land.

COLORS

The yellow-bellied sea snake is named for its bright yellow belly. This snake's colors are unlike any other snake. The upper half of its body is black. Its lower half is bright yellow. On the tail, the black and yellow pattern becomes rippled or barred.

Not all yellow-bellied sea snakes are black and yellow, however. Some are deep blue or brown on top and cream or light brown on the bottom. Others are completely yellow.

The yellow-bellied sea snake is very colorful compared to some other sea snakes.

The paddle-like tail of this yellow-bellied sea snake shows the banding pattern that is common to this species. Its bright yellow belly may serve as a warning that it is poisonous.

WHERE THEY LIVE

Yellow-bellied sea snakes spend their entire lives in the ocean. They do not like freshwater, and never enter inland rivers or lakes. These snakes cannot survive in extremely cold temperatures. They prefer water that is between 53 and 97 degrees Fahrenheit (12 and 36°C).

Yellow-bellied sea snakes are most plentiful in shallow waters over **continental shelves**. But, they can also be seen hundreds of miles from land. These snakes are graceful, rapid swimmers. However, they spend most of their time floating on the surface of the water.

Yellow-bellied sea snakes can also dive up to 50 feet (15 m) deep. And, they can spend more than an hour underwater. Some snakes can even hold their breath for more than three hours. They usually feed on the surface during the day and spend their nights on the ocean floor.

Ocean currents and winds send these snakes on adventures across the sea.

WHERE THEY ARE FOUND

Yellow-bellied sea snakes can also be found off the southern coast of California.

No other snakes have as large of a **habitat** as yellow-bellied sea snakes. These snakes live from the coast of eastern Africa to the coast of Japan. Their range also extends south to Australia.

Ocean currents sometimes carry yellow-bellied sea snakes eastward deep into the Pacific Ocean. There, they can be found near Hawaii and on the western shore of Central America. The yellow-bellied sea snake is the most widespread snake species in the world.

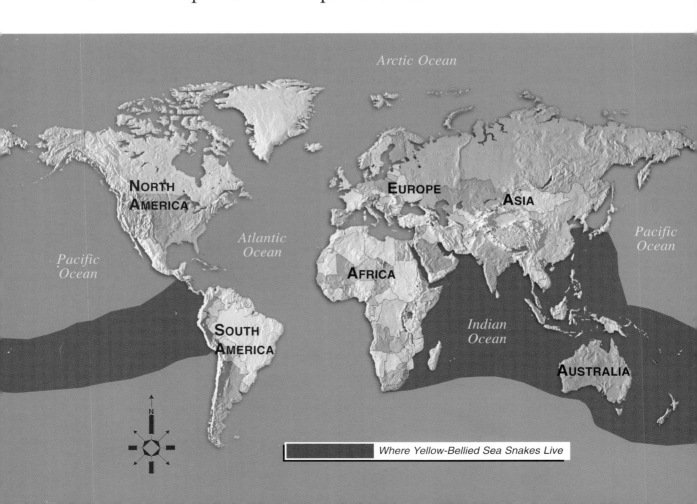

Where Yellow-Bellied Sea Snakes Live

SENSES

Yellow-bellied sea snakes spend their lives in salt water. They deal with different **environmental** conditions than land snakes. So, they have special senses adapted for sea life.

Too much salt can be unhealthy for any animal. Sea snakes need to regulate how much they absorb. So, they possess a special gland in their mouth under the tongue. The gland draws salt out of the water. This process helps keep a healthy balance of salt in the snakes.

Most snakes have nostrils on the front of their nose. But, sea snakes have their nostrils on the top of their nose. This makes breathing easier when they're floating in the ocean. When they dive, they can close their nose holes to keep the water out.

Sometimes, yellow-bellied sea snakes need to remain underwater for a long time. So, they are able to breathe through their skin. They do this by removing oxygen from the water and releasing carbon dioxide. This is called cutaneous breathing.

Unlike fish, sea snakes don't have gills. So, they must surface every couple of hours for air.

DEFENSE

The yellow-bellied sea snake's coloring is a warning sign to **predators**. Almost all animals avoid attacking this poisonous snake. Even birds and sharks stay away. Seabirds have been seen scooping them up out of the water but then quickly dropping them.

These snakes are not **aggressive**. They are only known to bite if harassed. But their **venom** is **neurotoxic**, and some scientists say it is even more poisonous than a cobra's! If you find one of these creatures on the beach, it is best to admire it from afar.

The biggest threat to the yellow-bellied sea snake is being stranded ashore. This sea snake will often die if it is not able to get back into the water. It also cannot survive in cold waters.

Occasionally yellow-bellied sea snakes end up on the beach. They are helpless on the shore.

FOOD

When looking for food, the sea snake floats on the surface of the water. It floats in the calm waters between ocean currents. This is where its prey is most common.

Small fish swim in these lanes. The fish feed on **plankton** and **larvae** that accumulate there.

The yellow-bellied sea snake waits until a fish swims near it. With a

Plankton blooming in the Atlantic Ocean can be seen from space. The plankton attracts the fish that the yellow-bellied sea snake feeds on.

swift, sideways swipe, the snake strikes its prey. **Venom** in the snake's bite works quickly to kill the fish. The yellow-bellied sea snake holds onto the fish until it stops wriggling. Once the fish is dead, the snake swallows it whole.

Depending on where they are, the yellow-bellied sea snake will eat different creatures. In addition to small fish, yellow-bellied sea snakes have also been known to eat eels.

BABIES

Many animals have certain times of the year when they mate. But, yellow-bellied sea snakes do not have a set mating period. These snakes mate on the surface of the ocean. The water temperature needs to be higher than 68 degrees Fahrenheit (20°C) for them to breed.

Normally these snakes live by themselves. But, they will group by the thousands when they are breeding. These groupings are called slicks. The slicks are often 10 feet (3 m) wide and 60 miles (97 km) long.

Female yellow-bellied sea snakes carry their eggs inside of them. It takes about five to six months for the eggs to fully develop. When they are ready, the eggs hatch inside of the mother. Soon after the eggs hatch, the mother snake will be ready to give birth to live young.

Mother yellow-bellied sea snakes give birth in the water. Typically, one to ten yellow-bellied sea snakes are born at a time. The babies are between 8 and 10 inches (20 and 25 cm) long.

Some sea snakes come ashore to lay their eggs. But, yellow-bellied sea snakes give birth at sea and never come ashore.

GLOSSARY

aggressive (uh-GREH-sihv) - displaying hostility.

alga - a plant or plantlike organism that lives mainly in the water.

barnacle - a crustacean that spends its adult life permanently attached to something, such as rocks, boats, or other marine animals.

continental shelf - a shallow, underwater plain that borders a continent and ends with a steep slope to the ocean floor.

environment - all the surroundings that affect the growth and well-being of a living thing.

family - a group that scientists use to classify similar plants or animals. It ranks above a genus and below an order.

habitat - a place where a living thing is naturally found.

larva - the early form of an animal, such as a frog, that must change before it is in its adult form.

neurotoxic - harmful to the nervous system of the body.

pelagic (puh-LA-jihk) - of or relating to the ocean.

plankton - small animals and plants that float in a body of water.

predator - an animal that kills and eats other animals.

venom - a poison produced by some animals and insects. It usually enters a victim through a bite or sting.

WEB SITES

To learn more about yellow-bellied sea snakes, visit ABDO Publishing Company on the World Wide Web at **www.abdopub.com**. Web sites about these snakes are featured on our Book Links page. These links are routinely monitored and updated to provide the most current information available.

INDEX

24